THE MARRIAGE LAW OF THE PEOPLE'S REPUBLIC OF CHINA

FOREIGN LANGUAGES PRESS BEIJING

First Edition 1982

ISBN 0-8351-1016-8

Published by the Foreign Languages Press
24 Baiwanzhuang Road, Beijing, China

Printed by the Foreign Languages Printing House
19 West Chegongzhuang Road, Beijing, China

Distributed by China Publications Centre (Guoji Shudian)
P.O. Box 399, Beijing, China

Printed in the People's Republic of China

CONTENTS

THE MARRIAGE LAW OF THE PEOPLE'S REPUBLIC OF CHINA

(Adopted by the Fifth National People's Congress at Its Third Session on September 10, 1980, and Put into Effect from January 1, 1981)

(Unofficial Translation)

CONTENTS

Chapter I

GENERAL PRINCIPLES

ARTICLE 1

This Law is the fundamental code governing marriage and family relations.

ARTICLE 2

The marriage system based on the free choice of partners, on monogamy and on equal rights for the sexes, is put into effect.

The lawful rights and interests of women, children and the aged are protected.

Family planning is practised.

ARTICLE 3

Marriage upon arbitrary decision by any third party, mercenary marriage and any other acts of interference in the freedom of marriage are prohibited. The exaction of money or gifts in connection with marriage is prohibited.

Bigamy is prohibited. Within the family maltreatment and desertion are prohibited.

Chapter II

MARRIAGE CONTRACT

ARTICLE 4

Marriage must be based upon the complete willingness of the two parties. Neither party shall use compulsion and no third party is allowed to interfere.

ARTICLE 5

No marriage shall be contracted before the man has reached 22 years of age and the woman 20 years of age. Late marriage and late childbirth should be encouraged.

ARTICLE 6

Marriage is not permitted in any of the following circumstances;

(1) where the man and woman are lineal relatives by blood or collateral relatives by blood (up to the third degree of relationship); and

(2) where one party is suffering from leprosy, a cure not having been effected, or from any other disease which is regarded by medical science as rendering a person unfit for marriage.

ARTICLE 7

Both the man and the woman desiring to contract a marriage shall register in person with the marriage registration office. If the proposed marriage is found to be in conformity with the provisions of this Law, registration shall be granted and a marriage certificate issued. The relationship of husband and wife is established when a marriage certificate is acquired.

ARTICLE 8

After a marriage has been registered, the woman may become a member of the man's family, or the man may become a member of the woman's family, according to the agreed wishes of the two parties.

Chapter III

FAMILY RELATIONS

ARTICLE 9

Husband and wife enjoy equal status in the home.

ARTICLE 10

Husband and wife each has the right to use his or her family name.

ARTICLE 11

Both husband and wife have the freedom to engage in production, to work, to study and to participate in social activities; neither party is allowed to restrain or interfere with the other.

ARTICLE 12

Husband and wife are in duty bound to practise family planning.

ARTICLE 13

The property acquired during the period in which husband and wife are under contract of marriage is in the joint possession of the two parties unless they have agreed otherwise.

Husband and wife enjoy equal rights in the management of the property in their joint possession.

ARTICLE 14

Husband and wife have the duty to support and assist each other.

When one party fails to perform this duty, the party in need of support and assistance has the right to demand that the other party pay the cost of support and assistance.

ARTICLE 15

Parents have the duty to rear and educate their children; children have the duty to support and assist their parents.

When parents fail to perform this duty, their children who are minors or who are not capable of living on their own have the right to demand that their parents pay for their care.

When children fail to perform the duty of supporting their parents, parents who have lost the ability to work or have difficulties in providing for themselves have the right to demand that their children pay for their support.

Infanticide by drowning and any other acts causing serious harm to infants are prohibited.

ARTICLE 16

Children may adopt either their father's or their mother's family name.

ARTICLE 17

Parents have the right and duty to subject their children who are minors to discipline and to protect them. When children who are minors have done harm to the state, to the collective, or to any other person, their parents are in duty bound to compensate for any economic loss.

ARTICLE 18

Husband and wife have the right to inherit each other's property.

Parents and children have the right to inherit each other's property.

ARTICLE 19

Children born out of wedlock enjoy the same rights as children born in lawful wedlock. No person shall harm them or discriminate against them.

The father of a child born out of wedlock must bear part or the whole of the cost of maintenance and education of the child until he or she can live on his or her own.

ARTICLE 20

The state protects lawful adoption. The relevant provisions in this Law governing the relations between parents and children are applicable to the rights and duties in the relations between adoptive parents and their adopted children.

The rights and duties in the relations between adopted children and their natural parents are terminated on the establishment of relationship of adoption.

ARTICLE 21

No maltreatment or discrimination is allowed between step-parents and their step-children.

The relevant provisions in this Law governing the relations between parents and children are applicable to the rights and duties in the relations between step-fathers or step-mothers and their step-children who receive care and education from their step-parents.

ARTICLE 22

Grandparents or maternal grandparents who have the capacity to bear the relevant costs have the duty to rear their grandchildren or maternal grandchildren who are minors and whose parents are deceased. Grandchildren or maternal grandchildren who have the capacity to bear the relevant costs have the duty to support and assist their grandparents or maternal grandparents whose children are deceased.

ARTICLE 23

Elder brothers or elder sisters who have the capacity to bear the relevant costs have the duty to rear their minor younger brothers or sisters whose parents either are deceased or have no capacity to rear them.

Chapter IV

DIVORCE

ARTICLE 24

Divorce is granted when husband and wife both desire it. Both parties should apply for divorce to the marriage registration office. The marriage registration office, after clearly establishing that divorce is desired by both parties and that appropriate measures have been taken for the care of any children and property, should issue the divorce certificate without delay.

ARTICLE 25

When one party insists on divorce, the organizations concerned may try to effect a reconciliation, or the party may appeal directly to the people's court for divorce.

In dealing with a divorce case, the people's court should try to bring about a reconciliation between the parties. In cases of complete alienation of mutual affection, and when mediation has failed, divorce should be granted.

ARTICLE 26

If the spouse of a member of the armed forces on active service insists on divorce, consent must be obtained from the member concerned.

ARTICLE 27

The husband is not allowed to apply for a divorce when his wife is pregnant or within one year after the birth of a child. This restriction does not apply in the case of the wife applying for divorce, or when the people's court deems it absolutely necessary to agree to deal with a divorce application by the husband.

ARTICLE 28

After divorce, if both parties desire to resume husband-and-wife relations, they should apply to the marriage registration office for a registration of remarriage. The marriage registration office should accept such a registration.

ARTICLE 29

The blood ties between parents and children are not ended by the divorce of the parents. Whether the father or the mother has the custody of the children, they remain the children of both parties.

After divorce, both parents continue to have the right and duty to rear and educate their children.

The guiding principle after divorce is to allow the mother to have the custody of a breast-fed infant. If a dispute arises between the two parties over the guardianship of a child after weaning and agreement cannot be reached, the people's court should make a judgement in accordance with the rights and interests of the child and the circumstances of both parties.

ARTICLE 30

If, after divorce, one party is given custody of a child, the other party is responsible for part or all of the necessary cost of the maintenance and education of the child. The two parties should reach an agreement regarding the amount of the cost and the duration of its payment for such maintenance and education. If such an agreement is lacking, the people's court should make a judgement.

An agreement reached between parents or a judgement made by the people's court in connection with the cost of the maintenance and education of a child does not obstruct the child from making a reasonable request where necessary for either parent to increase the amount decided upon by agreement or by judicial decision.

ARTICLE 31

In case of divorce, the disposal of the property in the joint possession of husband and wife is subject to agreement between the two parties. In cases where agreement cannot be reached, the people's court should make a judgement after taking into consideration the actual state of the family property and the rights and interests of the wife and the child or children.

ARTICLE 32

In case of divorce, debts incurred jointly by husband and wife during the period of their married life should be paid off out of their joint property. In cases where such property is insufficient to pay off such debts, the two parties should work out an agreement with regard to the payment; if an agreement cannot be reached, the people's court should make a judgement. Debts incurred separately by the husband or wife should be paid off by the party responsible.

ARTICLE 33

In case of divorce, if one party has maintenance difficulties, the other party should render appropriate financial assistance. Both parties should work out an agreement with regard to the details; in case an agreement cannot be reached, the people's court should make a judgement.

Chapter V
BY-LAWS

ARTICLE 34

Persons violating this Law shall be subject to administrative disciplinary measures or legal sanctions according to law and the circumstances.

ARTICLE 35

In cases where the relevant party refuses to execute judgements or rulings regarding maintenance, costs of upbringing or support, or regarding the division or inheritance of property, the people's court has the power to enforce their execution in accordance with the law. The organizations concerned have the duty to assist such execution.

ARTICLE 36

The people's congresses and their standing committees in national autonomous areas may enact certain modifications or supplementary articles in keeping with the principles of this Law and in conformity with the actual conditions prevailing among the minority nationalities of the locality in regard to marriage and family relations. But such provisions enacted by autonomous prefectures and autonomous counties must be submitted to the standing committee of the provincial or autonomous regional people's congress for ratification. Provisions enacted by autonomous regions must be submitted to the Standing Committee of the National People's Congress for the record.

ARTICLE 37

This Law comes into force from January 1, 1981.

The Marriage Law of the People's Republic of China promulgated on May 1, 1950 shall be repealed as of the date of the coming into force of this Law.

EXPLANATIONS ON THE MARRIAGE LAW (REVISED DRAFT) AND THE NATIONALITY LAW (DRAFT) OF THE PEOPLE'S REPUBLIC OF CHINA

— Given at the Third Session of the Fifth National People's Congress on September 2, 1980

Wu Xinyu, Vice-Chairman of the Commission for Legal Affairs of the Standing Committee of the National People's Congress

The Marriage Law (revised draft) and the Nationality Law (draft) of the People's Republic of China have been examined by the Standing Committee of the National People's Congress, which has decided that the two laws be submitted to the Third Session of the Fifth National People's Congress for examination. On behalf of the Commission for Legal Affairs of the Standing Committee of the National People's Congress, I am going to give the following explanations on the two draft laws:

1. CONCERNING THE MARRIAGE LAW OF THE PEOPLE'S REPUBLIC OF CHINA (REVISED DRAFT)

The present revised draft was drawn up on the basis of the Marriage Law of the People's Republic of China promulgated in 1950 and in the light of practical experience and the changing situation over the past thirty years by a revision group consisting of the All-China Women's Federation, the Supreme People's Court, the Supreme People's Procuratorate, the Ministry of Civil Affairs, the Ministry of Public Health, the Leading Family Planning Group, the State Nationalities Affairs Commission, the General Political Department of the People's Liberation Army, the All-China Federation of Trade

Unions and the Central Committee of the Communist Youth League of China.

In the course of revising the law, we had carried out widespread investigations and conducted three public opinion polls throughout the country. After discussion and revision by the Commission for Legal Affairs, the revised draft was then submitted to the Fourteenth Meeting of the Standing Committee of the National People's Congress for examination in April 1980, at which it was decided to print and distribute the draft to the standing committees of the people's congresses of the provinces, autonomous regions and municipalities directly under the Central Government, to the central departments concerned and to the Chinese People's Political Consultative Conference for their opinions. Taking into account their opinions, the Commission for Legal Affairs and the All-China Women's Federation revised the Law again and submitted it for examination to the Fifteenth Meeting of the Standing Committee of the National People's Congress.

The Marriage Law is the fundamental code governing marriage and family relations as well as an important law concerning the vital interests of each family and each person. The following are the main points of the draft law:

First, the legal age of marriage. The 1950 Marriage Law stipulated that "a marriage can be contracted only after the man has reached 20 years of age and the woman 18 years of age." The revised draft has changed the legal marriageable age to 22 for men and 20 for women, two years older than the age for both sexes in the 1950 law. The overwhelming majority of the provinces, autonomous regions, and centrally administered municipalities and the central departments approve of the revision and think that it is appropriate, because it has taken into consideration the actual situation in both urban and rural areas. People in some minority nationality regions and economically and culturally backward rural areas think that the marriageable age is too high and that it would be difficult to observe this provision. Taking into consideration the special conditions in the minority nationality areas, the draft law stipulates that the autonomous minority nationality regions may enact certain modifications or supplementary provisions in the light of the actual conditions prevailing among the minority nationalities of the locality in regard to marriage and family relations and in accordance with majority public opinion. In changing the custom of early marriage in the rural areas, we should continue our work of persuading the masses in step with the development of the rural economy and culture and encourage them gradually to implement the provision of their own accord. On the other hand, some people in urban areas think that the stipulated marriageable age-limit is too low and is contrary to the call for late marriage and for family planning. According to data from 31 countries throughout the world, the highest legal marriageable age-limit is 21 for men and 18 for women. But according to the 1950 Marriage Law China had the highest legal age for marriage. The legal marriageable age is the minimum age for marriage, that is, people should not get married below that age level. It does not mean that they have to get married on reaching that age. Our state has consistently encouraged young people to get married at an appropriate later age, in the belief that this benefits the state, the family as well as the individual. As to the effect the age for marriage has on family planning, it is crucial to separate marriage from childbirth, whilst promoting family planning. Therefore, the draft law stipulates: "Husband and wife are in duty bound to practise family planning," and "late marriage and late childbirth should be encouraged." So long as we do the work of family planning well, we shall control the growth of China's population. Otherwise, even if marriage takes place late, people can still give birth to many children. In some developed countries the legal age for marriage is generally quite low; in some countries in Western Europe, for example, 15 or 16 for women and 16, 18 or 21 for men — their population for many years has not basically increased but is actually decreasing. It proves that the legal age for marriage and controlling population growth are two different problems. Therefore, after the promulgation of the Marriage Law, we must continue to educate the people and pay attention to family planning. A programme for family planning should be formulated as soon as possible.

Second, divorce. The 1950 Marriage Law stipulated that: "In the event of either the husband or the wife alone insisting upon divorce, it may be granted only when mediation by the district people's government and the judicial organ has failed to bring about a reconciliation." This provision is still appropriate. In socialist China, it has always been advocated that a husband and wife should help each other and work towards a democratic and harmonious way of life within the family. It is necessary to promote communist morality and oppose rash decisions in marriage or the bourgeois ideology of loving the new and detesting the old. However, we cannot hope to preserve by legal means a genuinely broken marriage, which may cause long-term suffering to both parties, intensify the conflict or lead to homicide, and ultimately bring harm to society, the family and the parties concerned. As it is not long since the abolition of the feudal marriage and our economic and cultural level remains rather low, a section of public opinion is usually not sympathetic to the party who asks for a divorce. The problem is rather complicated, which was reflected in the fact that for many years the courts were too strict in handling divorce cases. On the basis of suggestions made by some local governments and departments, the draft law has revised the relevant provision to read: "In cases of complete alienation of mutual affection, and when mediation has failed, divorce should be granted," with the addition of the condition "in cases of complete alienation of mutual affection." The revised provision upholds the principles of freedom of marriage and at the same time provides the courts with a certain amount of flexibility to conform to the actual situation in China today.

Third, the right to inherit property. There are now more and more inheritance disputes, moreover they are rather complicated. The draft law cannot give detailed stipulations, only the principles: "Husband and wife have the right to inherit each other's property" and "parents and children have the right to inherit each other's property." Concrete questions can be included in future civil or inheritance law.

Fourth, the prohibition of marriage between collateral relatives by blood. The 1950 Marriage Law stipulated: "The question of prohibiting marriage between collateral relatives by blood (up to the fifth degree of relationship) is determined by custom." Many local governments and departments proposed that the revised law stipulate in clear-cut terms the prohibition of marriage between close relations, since marriages between collateral relatives by blood often produce children with congenital defects. Moreover, now that family planning is being promoted and the number of children is reduced, it is even more important to pay attention to the quality of the population. As a result, the revised law prohibits marriage between collateral relatives by blood (up to the third degree of relationship), including marriage between cousins who have the same paternal or maternal grandparents. Because of certain traditional customs, especially in certain remote mountainous areas this provision should be implemented gradually. Crude and summary methods should not be used.

Fifth, the question of the husband becoming a member of the wife's family. The revised law stipulates that "the woman may become a member of the man's family, or the man may become a member of the woman's family, according to the agreed wishes of the two parties."

This provision will help to guarantee the freedom of marriage, promote family planning, and solve the practical difficulties of families who have daughters but no sons. The clause does not mention "making one's domicile" because it refers to becoming a member of one's spouse's household, but not to transferring one's legal place of domicile. A change in the legal place of domicile requires other procedures which are not necessarily linked with marriage. If, upon agreement, one party becomes a member of the other party's family, he or she should enjoy the rights and undertake the duties of a member of that family. Even if one party's legal place of domicile is not where the other party lives, he or she has the duty to support the old people and also enjoys the right to inherit property.

Sixth, because the customs and habits of some minority nationalities are different from those of the Han regions and because their economic and cultural levels are also different, the draft law stipulates that in areas where minority nationalities enjoy autonomy certain modifications and supplementary provisions may be made in accordance with the principles of this law and taking into account the actual marriage and family circumstances of the local minorities.

Seventh, because publicity should be given to the revised law to prepare the people for its implementation, it has been suggested that the revised law come into effect from January 1, 1981, after it has been examined and approved for promulgation by the Session.

2. CONCERNING THE NATIONALITY LAW OF THE PEOPLE'S REPUBLIC OF CHINA (DRAFT)

(This section is omitted here. — Editor.)

The above drafts of the two laws are submitted to the Session for examination and approval for promulgation.

中华人民共和国婚姻法

*

外文出版社出版
（中国北京百万庄路24号）
外文印刷厂印刷
中国国际书店发行
（北京399信箱）
1982年（32开）第一版
编号：（英）6050—35
00025
6—E—1676P